JACQUES-HENRI LARTIGUE

Jacques-Henri Lartigue

Introduction by Jacques Damade

PANTHEON BOOKS, NEW YORK

CENTRE NATIONAL DE LA PHOTOGRAPHIE, PARIS

On the cover: Grand Prix de l'A.C.F., Automobile Delage, 1912.

Library of Congress Cataloging-in-Publication Data.

Lartigue, Jacques-Henri, 1894-
Jacques-Henri Lartigue.

Translated from the French.
Bibliography: p.

1. Lartigue, Jacques-Henri, 1894-
2. Photography, Artistic. I. Centre national
de la photographie (France)   II. Title.
TR653.L37813   1986   779'.092'4   86-18764
ISBN 0-394-74781-X (pbk.)

Manufactured in Italy/First American Edition.

ADVENTURING INTO THE FAMILIAR

In one of the first entries he made in his journal, Jacques Lartigue describes photography in a completely unexpected way: he speaks of "mysterious smells, a bit bizarre and frightening, that one quickly learns to like." Presumably, the youthful Lartigue is talking about the various chemical operations involved in developing and printing photographs; indeed, it is easy to imagine how rich in smells and sensations - both new and vaguely disturbing for a child - photography can be: purchasing the glass plates wrapped in nice black paper at the optician's, handling them, and developing them in the darkroom. It is, however, more tempting to see in this shift of sense a sort of synthesis at work, i.e., that one sense appears, consciously or not, to symbolize another. Moreover, it must be noted that in the scale of perceptive senses, smell gives an idea of greater closeness and intimacy than sight, and, along with touch, is the one most connected with the body. Such preeminence of smell over sight is paradoxical in a photographer and is indicative of the close link that Lartigue had with what he photographed, namely an emotional, natural link, an assimilation moving from close to closer. The photographic eye does not just see; it is even closer than that. It does not just capture a shape; it grasps the "mysterious smells." As Avedon wrote about Lartigue, "His photos are almost palpable."

Born at the turn of the century into a wealthy bourgeois family, Jacques Lartigue would later become the chronicler of this period. He began to take pictures when he was very young, recounting his family's unfolding history from the point of view of a child learning to understand, to marvel, and to grow. Along with taking photos, he kept a journal and sketched lively little drawings of scenes he was afraid he had missed with his camera. He employed a number of methods that recorded, grasped, and preserved the principal things that happened before his eyes. Lartigue used them with the full pleasure of an amateur, with no other need than to capture and save the happy moments of his family, their lives and the movement of their bodies. Photography, writing, sketching - three different and complementary ways to fashion a second memory, a unique family album that by its size and scope (250,000 photos and countless journals) tends to substitute for memory.

The subjects of his photographs always have a corporal link with his existence, and permeating his pictures are these "mysterious smells" of intimacy. The pleasures of the Lartigue clan seem naive, specific, and numerous. Not happy simply to take pictures, he compiled his photos, dating them and organizing them as one would a herbarium. He pursued this slow exercise with the passion of a collector whose collection is composed of the instants of his own life, barely detached from him, over with yet still present, forever fixed and classified.

Up until the 1960s, Lartigue considered photography as a secondary activity, a hobby. It was not until 1963 that an exhibition of his work was organized for the first time at the Modern Art Museum of New York. Prior to this, Lartigue's work had remained private, even if now and then a few shrewd connoisseurs had published certain photos. His work had evolved sheltered from attention, in a highly personal way; and, it is interesting to note that exhibiting did not change the situation in any absolute way. Indeed, along with achieving recognition so late in life – Lartigue was sixty-nine – he became known essentially for his work between 1900-1930, i.e., a period which does not correspond to his photographic work at the time he was discovered. In this way, he was able to pursue his current work more or less in private, while being known by a vast public for his photos of the early 1900s. It was as if history, with its customary off-beat rhythm and irony, continued to protect his work from the public eye. Perhaps having kept amateur status for so long nurtured his greatest attribute: he never renounced the intimacy of his subjects, and the camera was never an abstract eye indiscriminately recording any reality it came upon.

Sprinkled throughout his albums are short marginal notes. These infrequent notes are invaluable because they indicate the directions he took and his bearings, like milestones on the path he followed as a photographer.

Next to one picture he wrote, "An idea: take a picture of Bichonnade and Mama when they are wearing nice hats." There follows a shot of the two smiling women, wearing incredible garden hats. On the same page, lower down, next to another photo: "Another idea: suppose I go to the park to photograph the ladies wearing the most outrageous or beautiful hats!" A series follows of photos of women strolling in the Bois de Boulogne, wearing hats decorated with ostrich feathers, plumes, veils, fox tails, doves, bunches of grapes, and so on. The theme unfolds sequentially; it is a story without words, as amusing as a silent movie, with a beginning, a middle, and an end. Lartigue's annotations illustrate his working procedure. He operated by a method of successive assimilation, starting from his most immediate environment and following through in a line of continuous variation: first his mother's hat, then those of the ladies strolling in the Bois de Boulogne. Several pages farther on, Lartigue writes: "The fashionable people amuse me and I am going to photograph them in the park and at the races." His work consists of concentric circles, ever widening without the slightest break. His way of using the private as a stepping stone to the public is inherent, almost natural; it is evidenced by the pictures of pedal cars, Zissou's wagons, his father's Panhard Levassor, and the car races of the Grand Prix of the Automobile Club of France.

The continuum makes it possible to eliminate, by nearly imperceptible gradations, divisions that are too clear-cut, such as private and public, or child and adult. The most blatant characteristic in Lartigue's photographic themes is the interrelationships among his subjects; like a sound wave, they ripple along the same line: cars, and flying objects, toys, kites, *aviettes* (bicycles equipped with wings, used at the turn of the century), airplanes, etc. His is the art of crossing borders, categories, of opening up spaces without forcing anything at all.

After 1890, Jacob Riis published a book entitled *How the Other Half Lives,* in which he concentrated on the poor neighborhoods of New York, on their appearance and the atmosphere of despair. Unlike Lartigue, Jacob Riis was separate from his subject. The difference is absolute, and he is part of a dual sadness: that of portraying unhappiness and poverty and that of being exiled from it. That radical separation between photographers and their subjects typifies more the general trend in photography than the closeness maintained by Jacques Lartigue. It is therefore not surprising that he occupies a place apart in the evolution of photography.

On his seventh birthday, Lartigue wrote about his gift in his journal: "My camera is made of polished wood with a bellows made of red-bordered green fabric, in accordion pleats. It fits in a large box with all the accessories. A tripod taller than I, also in wood. Frames to hold large, greenish-yellow plates wrapped in beautiful black paper, which I was quite wrong to unwrap in the light. And all sorts of things too complicated and heavy for a little boy only 1.20 meters tall." Although, in the beginning, the young Lartigue took pictures only of his room, his parents, his nurse Dudu, and his garden, using these heavy and fragile plates to take possession of his immediate universe, his tripod camera very quickly enlarged this circle. Not content to make an inventory of what was undisputably his world, he sought to capture the movement of the outdoor games with his big brother Zissou, Bichonnade, and his friends. Little by little, the cameras changed, until he acquired a snapshot camera like the Spido Gaumont. His perception grew sharper and he became more mobile, which allowed him to photograph subjects in full flight, or on the run ("My cat Zizi," 1904).

Jacques Lartigue grew up in the company of folding cameras, tripods, and sensitive plates. This company was not without consequence, for his evolving cognizance of the world and the discovery of space had a dual aspect: that of himself, his body, his childish awkwardness and explorations and that of his photographic eye, the darkroom where distance is discovered, accommodating itself to space. The cameras in those days were no longer the heavy, old-fashioned aparatus of Daguerre's days, weighing between fourty and ninety pounds, requiring minutes of immobility in a glass house in full sunshine. However, focusing had to be exact, so it was necessary to evaluate space with the precision of a surveyor.

Far from dodging the difficult problem of space, Lartigue made it the center of his concerns, displaying a surprising perfectionism. Speaking about one of the walks in the Bois de Boulogne, he writes in his journal, "It's there that I am on the lookout, sitting in a wrought-iron chair, my camera already focused. Distance: 4 – 5 meters; speed: curtain opening: 4 mm. Diaphragm: that depends on what side 'she' will come from. I can judge distance at a glance. What is not so easy is to position myself exactly at the right spot so 'she' takes a step forward just at the moment when the focus setting is perfect." Estimating distance, calculating light and depth of field, and especially putting himself in the right place – all these actions, repeated thousands of times over from the time he was a child, sharpened and strengthened the young man's depth perception. What is striking about him is the extremely lively attention he gave to movements and their drollery. He had an intuitive sense of shooting at the most precise moment of the gesture. The acrobatic positions he assumed audaciously competed with what he was photographing – lying on his stomach in a high bed of gravel to get Zissou's wagon taking a turn, jumping from a chair at Rouzat in a jackknife. Asking oneself where the photographer was when he took the shot adds another dimension of humor to the picture.

That life of movement implies more than simple mastery: it is a moment of grace and happiness; it is the exploring that opens the child's body to the distance from the world, offering him an immensity, an expansion, and an extraordinary liberty. So many pictures are just so many windows on the sky, the outdoors. Never has a family circle seemed so wide, in full expansion, aerated, airborne, as the one depicted on Lartigue's rectangle of photographic paper.

Contrary to the usual family photos, where the mother and the father are shown in the framework of respectable intimacy, where images prudently trace tangible frontiers with the outside, defining a family tree with its branches, marriages, and descendants, where identity is the major concern, Lartigue's youthful pictures deliberately focus on the exploits and adventures of his relatives. Wagons, cars, skating, kites, airplanes, races. Sometimes, as if the movement were insufficient, or the camera speed not fast enough, the lines are blurred and obstacles disappear, giving way to the beach or the sky "without anything weighing down or striking a pose." "The beach," he wrote in his journal, "is the most immense place on earth. You can run there 'without bounds,' and no one will cry out to you to be careful. Nothing hinders my eyes more from roaming or from drifting endlessly." Less well known, but nevertheless numerous, are his panoramic views, with people in the foreground taken from the back, in profile, in silhouette; black spots on a white background, contemplating the horizon, or a flying object of some kind, creating an impression of depth. Dreamy, almost meditative in the fullest sense of the word, these pictures seem to correspond to what Bachelard termed in The *Poétique of Space* the "intimate immensity": "When he really lives the word 'immense,' the dreamer sees himself liberated from his cares, his thoughts, liberated from his dreams. He is no longer constrained by his own weight. He is no longer a prisoner of his own being."

Jacques-Henri Lartigue's photographs are of those priviliged moments that make the intimate family circle ripple, expand, and open up to the cosmos in a gradual, almost natural way. Lartigue teaches us to see the adventure in the familiar. He does not renounce the "mysterious smells" of photography. He combines, the intimacy of his subject with openness and expansion. Lartigue was a happy moralist, telling us that truth that family pictures, imprisoned in their frames, generally ignore: there is no closeness without space.

Jacques Damade
Translated by Marianne Tinnell Faure

1. Bois de Boulogne, Grandmother, Mother, and myself, 1903.

2. My garden, Pont de l'Arche, 1904.

3. My nanny Dudu, Paris, 1904.

4. Zissou, Robert, Louis and I, Pont de l'Arche, 1903.

5. Paris, 1905.

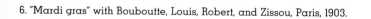

6. "Mardi gras" with Bouboutte, Louis, Robert, and Zissou, Paris, 1903.

7. My cat Zizi, Paris, 1904.

8. My uncle, Auguste, Dédé, Marcelle. Pont de l'Arche, 1903.

9. Toboggan, Luna Park, 1909.

10. James and Rico, Rouzat, 1910.

11. Bouboutte, Rouzat, 1908.

12. Marcelle's first communion, Le Mans, 1907.

13. Races at Auteuil, 1911.

14. Charity day for the wounded, Vichy, 1915.

15. Marthe Chenal at the Racing Club de France, 1916.

16. Model plane trial at the Trocadero, 1908.

17. The ZYX 21, Zissou, Rouzat, 1908.

18. The ZYX 24 takes off Piroux, Zissou, Georges, Louis, Dédé, and Robert try to take off with it, Rouzat, 1910.

19. The airplane *Antoinette,* 1910.

20. Maurice Farman in his biplane, Le Buc, 1911

21. Deauville, 1919

22. Guitty (Marguerite Bourcart) in Biarritz, 1905

23. Zissou. Voisin's airplane, Merlimont, 1904

24. The glider *Archdeacon* before departure, Merlimont, 1904

25. Cousin Caro and M. Plantevigne, Villerville, 1906

26. Kite, Biarritz, 1905

27. Zissou at the Adour bore, Biarritz, 1909

28. Trip to in Auvergne, Automobile 22HP Peugeot, 1910

29. Circuit of Auvergne. The famous Mercedes by Jenatzy, 1905

30. Circuit of Auvergne, my "famous heroes" Duray
sur Lorraine-Dietrich, 1905

31. The A.C.F. Grand Prix. The great runner Nazzaro
signals Wagner to speed up, 1912

32. Gaillon, 1912

33. Gaby Deslys. Scene at the Casino de Paris
during the film *Bouclette,* 1918

34. Horse races at Auteuil, 1911

35. Avenue des Acacias, Paris, 1911

36. Avenue du Bois de Boulogne, 1911

37. Horse races at Montreuil, 1911

38. World Championships at St Cloud.
The German champion Froitzeim, 1913

39. The champion Géo André, Paris, 1924

40. Buffalo cycling stadium, Paris, 1908

41. Paris-Tours motorcycle race, Orléans, 1912

42. Race at Cap d'Antibes, 1929

43. Grand Prix auto race, La Baule, 1929

44. The Duke of Monpensier's wedding, Rendan, 1921

45. Solange, Neuilly, 1929

46. Bibi at the exhibition of 1925, Paris, 1925

47. Dancing, Vichy, 1922

48. Automobile Hispano Suiza 32HP, on the road to Houlgate
with Mamie, Bibi, and Jean the chauffeur, 1927

49. "Feu de Baroncelli", Chouchou, Epinay, 1926

50. Guston Ravel shooting *Le roman d'un jeune homme pauvre,* Royan, 1926

51. Renée in Ciboure, 1930

52. Bibi in Marseille, 1928

53. René Bolloré, Denise Grey, and Bibi on the Atlantic Ocean, 1926

54. Loulou and Pierre Boucard pass us in their Rolls-Royce, Royan, 1926

55. Rocher de la Vierge. Sala, Biarritz, 1927

56. Renée in Biarritz. Swimmingpool called "Chambre d'Amour," 1930

57. The "Grande Côte." Bibi and Grete, Royan, 1926

58. Italian border. Luigi, street-singer, 1927

59. Storm. Bibi, Irène, Arlette, Cannes, 1929

60. Storm in Nice, 1925

61. Biarritz, 1931

62. San Sebastian Beach, 1928

63. Trouville, 1923

BIOGRAPHY

1894. Jacques-Henri Lartigue born on June 13 at Courbevoie. Received his first camera at age 7 (a 13 x 18 tripod box camera) from his father, a businessman and an avid amateur photographer.

About 1900. Lartigue begins keeping the journal that he will continue all his life. In it he gives quick descriptions and impressions of his daily activities and family life, and precise sketches of what he has photographed.

Also starts keeping his photo albums. Today there are 116 of them, containing 200,000 prints.

1902. Lartigue takes his first photos by himself. He quickly becomes interested in movement, and as soon as he attains the technical ability, begins to take his first action shots (jumps, ball games, tennis, etc). Often uses as models his brother Zissou and his cousins at play at Pont de l'Arche and at the Château de Rouzat. Other favorite subjects are airplanes, automobiles, and the beautifully dressed ladies strolling in the Bois de Boulogne.

1915. Enters the Académie Julian. Studies under Jean-Paul Laurens, Decheneau, Baschet.

1919. Marries Bibi Messager, daughter of André Messager, composer, conductor, and general manager of the Opéra.

1922. Exhibits at the Salon d'Automne and at the salon of the Société Nationale des Beaux-Arts at the Grand Palais. Begins his career as a painter.

1932. Very much interested in filmmaking, becomes set photographer for the film *Le Roi Pausole* and also serves as assistant director.

1935. Between 1935 and 1950, works as an illustrator for fashion magazines.

Establishes a reputation as decorator for galas held in Cannes, La Baule, and Lausanne.

1942. Marries Florette Orméa.

From 1950. His photographs appear more and more often in the press, particularly in Catholic papers. His photos of Picasso are published the world over.

1954. Creation of the Association "Gens d'Images"; holds office of vice-president. Exhibits as part of the association along with other photographers at the Galerie d'Orsay in 1955 and 1956, and is a regular member of the jury for the Niepce Award.

1963. The exhibition at the Museum of Modern Art in New York in 1963 and a 10-page article in *Life* (November) mark the real starting points of the artistic career of Lartigue the photographer. Charles Rado, from the Rado Agency, shows his photos to John Szarkowski, director of the photography department of the museum of Modern Art, who sees in him "the precursor of all that was alive and interesting during the middle of the 20th century."

1966. Publication of *Family Album.* The international edition contributes greatly to making his work more well known.

1970. Publication of *Diary of a Century (Moments from My Life).* Conceived by Richard Avedon, this book reveals for the first time photos taken after 1930.

1975. The first retrospective of his work entittled "Lartigue 8 x 80," Is held in France at the Musée des Arts Décoratifs.

1979. On June 26, officially donates the entirety of his photographic works to France.

BIBLIOGRAPHY

1963. The Photographs of Jacques-Henri Lartigue
Catalogue of the exhibition held at the Museum of Modern Art in New York. Introduction by John Szarkowski.

1966. Les photographies de J.-H. Lartigue
A family album from the "Belle Epoque," presented by Jean Fondin. Ami-Guichard Edita, Lausanne, 1966.

English edition, **Boyhood Photos of J.-H. Lartigue, The Family Album of a Gilded Age,** Guichard, Time-Life Books, New York, 1966.

1970. Diary of a Century
Work designed and with an introduction by Richard Avedon Viking Press, New York. Weidenfeld & Nicholoson, London, 1971.

German edition: **Photo-Tagebuch unseres Jahrhunderts.** Bücher Verlag, Lucerne, 1971.

French edition: **Instants de ma vie.** Editions du Chêne, Paris, 1973.

1972. Portfolio J.-H. Lartigue Ten original, signed photographs by J.-H. Lartigue, edition limited to 50 copies. Introduction by Anaïs Nin. Editions Witkin-Berley Ltd., New York.

1973. Lartigue et les femmes Photographs and notes by J.-H. Lartigue.
Editions du Chêne, Paris.
Studio Vista, London, 1974.
Dutton & Co., New York, 1974.

1973. Das Fest des Grossen Rüpüskul
Text by Elisabeth Borchers.
Photographs by J.-H. Lartigue.
Insel Verlag, Frankfurt am Main.

1974. J.-H. Lartigue et les autos
Photographs and notes by J.-H Lartigue.
Editions du Chêne, Paris.

1975. Mémoires sans mémoire
Excepts from the journal of J.-H. Lartigue.
Editions Robert Laffont, Paris.

1975. Lartigue 8 x 80
Catalogue of the exposition organized by the CCI (Centre de Création Industrielle) and the Public Relations office of Kodak Pathé at the Musée des Arts Décoratifs in Paris.
Delpire Editeur, Paris.

1976. Histoire de la photographie J.-H. Lartigue
Nouvel Observateur/Delpire. Published simultaneously by Aperture Inc., New York, and Delpire Editeur, Paris.

1977. Mon livre de photographie
Editions du Chat Perché, Flammarion, Paris.

1978. Drei Klassiken der Fotografie: Lartigue, Kertesz, Steichen
Edited by Rogner Bernhard.

1978. Portfolio J.-H. Lartigue 1903-1916
Signed edition, 7, 500 copies.
10 photographs. Time-Life Books.

1980. Les Femmes aux cigarettes
96 photographs and preface by J.-H. Lartigue. Designed and produced by Sheldom Cother Inc.
The Viking Press, New York.

1980. Les autochromes de J.-H. Lartigue 1912-1927
Editions Herscher, Paris.
Swan Verlag (Germany), 1981.
Viking Press (USA), 1981.
Ash Grant (Great Britain), 1981.

1980. Bonjour Monsieur Lartigue
Exhibition catalogue edited by "L'Association des Amis de Jacques-Henri Lartigue," Paris.

1981. Jacques-Henri Lartigue
by Henry Chapier. Collection "Les grands photographes."
Belfond, Paris.

1981. L'émerveillé. Ecrit à mesure
1923-1931. Excerpts from the journal of Jacques-Henri Lartigue.
Editions Stock, Paris.

EXHIBITIONS

1955. Galerie d'Orsay. First presentation of photographs by J.-H Lartigue.

1963. First exhibition devoted entirely to Lartigue. Organized by John Szarkowski, at the Museum of Modern Art, New York.

1966. Important exhibition at the Photokina in Cologne.

1969. Festival d'Avignon, France.

1971. Several photographs by Lartigue presented at the exhibition "Récents enrichissements des collections photographiques du cabinet des Estampes," on the occasion of the opening of a photography gallery at the Bibliothèque Nationale, Paris.

1971. Exhibition at the Photographer's Gallery of London.
From 1971 to 1973, this exhibition traveled throughout England.

In France:
La Vieille Charité, Marseille, 1972;
Théâtre de l'Hôtel de Ville, Le Havre, 1972.

In Germany:
Museum für Kunst und Gewerbe, Hamburg, 1972.

1972. Exhibition at the Neikrug Gallery and the Witkin Gallery in New York. This dual exhibition was later acquired by the Cinémathèque in Quebec for the Bibliothèque Nationale de Montréal.

1973. Participated in numerous collective exhibitions, in particular in Dijon at the "Confrontation 73," at Carmel, California, and at the annual Festival in Birmingham, Alabama.

1974. Center of Photographic Art, Chicago.

1975. Galerie Optica, Montreal. This exhibition was subsequently mounted at Loretta Yarlow Fine Arts, Toronto;

French Institute/Alliance Française, New York;
The Visual Studies Workshop Gallery, Rochester;
The Art Gallery of Ontario;
Columbia College, Chicago;
The International Center of Photography, New York.

1975. Witkin Gallery, New York.

1975. "Lartigue 8 x 80." Exhibition presented by the Centre National d'Art et de Culture Georges Pompidou, and the Public Relations office of Kodak Pathé, at the Musée des Arts Décoratifs in Paris. This exhibition, comprising 200 large-format photographs was the first big retrospective in France of Lartigue's work in photography. It was also mounted at:
Europalia 75 France, Ghent, Antwerp;
Van Gogh Museum, Amsterdam;
Galerie Fiolet, Amsterdam;
Centre d'Action Culturelle, Mâcon (1976);
Chambéry (1976);
Maison Européenne de la Photographie, Châlon-sur-Saône (1976).

1975. Municipal gallery at the Château d'Eau, Toulouse.

1975. Festival d'Arles.

1975. Participation in collective exhibitions at:
Maison de la Culture Ibn Rachid, Tunis;
"Audiovisuel Lartigue," Centre Georges Pompidou, Paris;
"Cent Ans de Couleurs," Salon de la Photographie, Paris; "The Land: 20th Century Landscape" photographs selected by Bill Brandt. This exhibition was also presented at the Victoria and Albert Museum in London, followed by the National Gallery of Modern Art in Edinburgh; the Ulster Museum in Belfast; and the National Museum of Wales in Cardiff.

1976. Schiedams Museum, Holland.
Arnhems Museum, Holland.

1977. "Photographie Créative du XXe siècle," Centre Georges Pompidou, Paris (group exhibition).

1977. Centre de la Part Dieu, Lyon.

1978. Palais de l'Europe, Menton (photographs and paintings).

1980. Olympus Gallery, London.

1980. "Bonjour Monsieur Lartigue" exhibition mounted by the "Association des Amis de Jacques-Henri Lartigue" in conjunction with the national heritage year and in cooperation with the Ministry of Culture and Communication Galeries Nationales du Grand Palais, Paris. Comprising 155 photographs, this exhibition was organized as a tribute to the donation by Lartigue to France of the whole of his photographic work. The exhibition was also shown at the Fondation Nationale de la Photographie in Lyon.

1981. Opening of an exhibition hall at the Grand Palais (Avenue Winston Churchill), with a permanent exhibition of 80 photographs.
At the same time, the following temporary exhibitions were held:
- Sacha Guitry et Yvonne Printemps;
- Paysages;
- Tennis 1910-1926.

1982. International Center of Photography in New York. Presentation of a new version of the exhibition "Bonjour Monsieur Lartigue." This exhibition of 125 photographs traveled throughout the United States for three years.

FILMS

1966. Le Magicien
Directed by Claude Fayard. Produced by Coty.

1970. La famille Lartigue
Directed by Robert Hugues. Produced by the O.R.T.F. for the series "Panorama."

1971-1972. Jacques-Henri Lartigue
Directed by Claude Ventura. Produced by the O.R.T.F. for the series "Italiques."

1980. Jacques-Henri Lartigue, un photographe
Directed by Fernand Moscovitz. Produced by the Ministry of Foreign Affairs.

1980-81. Jacques-Henri Lartigue, peinture et photographe
Directed by François Reichenbach. Produced by A2, in four episodes.

PANTHEON PHOTO LIBRARY

American Photographers of the Depression
Eugène Atget
Henri Cartier-Bresson
Bruce Davidson
Early Color Photography
Robert Frank
André Kertész
Jacques-Henri Lartigue
Duane Michals
The Nude
W. Eugene Smith
Weegee

The Pantheon Photo Library:
a collection conceived and produced by the
National Center of Photography in Paris
under the direction of Robert Delpire.